REGIONS OF THE WORLD

The United States and Canada

Revised Edition

Mark Stewart

capstone

a division of Capstone Global Library, LLC.
Chicago, Illinois

Customer Service 800-747-4992
Visit our Web site at: www.mycapstone.com

Editorial: Andrew Farrow
Design: Steve Mead and Q2A Creative
Illustrations: International Mapping Associates, Inc
Picture Research: Melissa Allison and Kay Altwegg
Production: Alison Parsons

Library of Congress Cataloging-in-Publication data is available on the Library of Congress website.

ISBN 978-1-4846-3814-9 (revised paperback)
ISBN 978-1-4846-3900-9 (ebook pdf)

Acknowledgments
The author and publishers are grateful to the following for permission to reproduce copyrighted material:

Alamy: Cultura Creative, 48, epa european pressphoto agency b.v., 51, Jeff Greenberg 6 of 6, 40, P.A. Lawrence, LLC., 25, RosalreneBetancourt 2, 41; Capstone Press: (map) 1, (map outline) throughout; Newscom: Adriana Zehbrauskas/Polaris/, 44, Ariel Skelley Blend Images, 32, DDAA/ZOB/Daniel Deme/WENN, 30, Evo/REX, 16, Images Distribution/Agence Quebec Presse, 26, Jean B. Heguy, 38, JORGE DUENES/REUTERS, 37, MICHAEL GIBSON/KRT, 39, Natan Dvir/Polaris, 27, Raffi Kirdi/Polaris, 29, REBECCA COOK/Reuters, 55, Roland Hemmi, 9, RON CORTES/KRT, 42, Stefan Wackerhagen imageBROKER, 10; North Wind Picture Archives, 4; Shutterstock: Andrew Bertino, 17, Arianna Tonarelli, cover, dikobraziy, 13, gpointstudio, 53, iofoto, 52, kan_khampanya, 21, KENNY TONG, 14, Laura Bartlett, 19, littleny, 33, marekuliasz, 22, Michael Dechev, 47, Oscity, 34, Rainer Lesniewski, 7

Printed and bound in the USA
PO9878R

Contents

Introducing the United States and Canada 5

Natural Features 11

People 23

Culture 35

Natural Resources and Economy 45

Fact File 56

Timeline 58

Glossary 60

Find Out More 62

Index 64

Any words appearing in the text in bold, **like this**, are explained in the glossary.

Introducing the United States and Canada

Canada and the United States of America are part of the North American landmass, which stretches from the Pacific Ocean in the west to the Atlantic Ocean in the east. To the north of Canada, and the U.S. state of Alaska, is the Arctic Ocean. To the south of these countries is the country of Mexico and the Gulf of Mexico. The Hawaiian Islands, America's 50th state, are located in the Pacific Ocean more than 2,000 miles (3,200 kilometers) off the mainland. From a geographer's standpoint, they are considered part of Oceania.

The United States and Canada lie between the North Pole and the **Tropic of Cancer**, the dividing line between the tropics and the cooler subtropic region. The U.S. covers 3.79 million square miles (9.82 million square kilometers). Canada is even larger, 3.85 million square miles (9.98 million square kilometers). Together the two countries make up more than four-fifths of North America. Mexico makes up the rest.

Canada is the second largest country in the world, after Russia, and the U.S. is third. Land in the U.S. and Canada is densely populated in some places and sparsely populated in others. The U.S. has about nine times as many people as Canada. Who lives where, why they live there, what they do, and how they got there has much to do with the climate, geography, and natural resources of the region. This book looks at how these themes combine to create one of the most diverse and dynamic places on Earth.

← The War of 1812, waged between the United States and Great Britain (with Canada on Britain's side), lasted from 1812 to 1815. It ended with the Treaty of Ghent, with neither side claiming victory. The United States and Canada are now close neighbors culturally as well as geographically.

Population of the United States and Canada

More than 330 million people currently live in the United States and Canada. That is almost equal to the combined populations of Great Britain, France, Germany, Italy, Spain, and Poland. The population of the U.S. and Canada is expected to continue to grow. Some of this growth will come from families already living in the region, and some will come from people who decide to make the United States or Canada their new home. The opportunity to live and work in a free society has always been appealing to people struggling in other lands. Indeed, the story of this region is tied very closely to the story of **immigration**.

In 2006, the population of the U.S. grew to more than 300 million. Its largest cities are New York City (8.1 million), Los Angeles (3.8 million), Chicago (2.9 million), Houston (2.0 million), Philadelphia (1.5 million), Phoenix (1.4 million), San Diego (1.2 million), San Antonio (1.2 million), and Dallas (1.2 million). New York City is the world's twelfth most populous city. It has about the same number of residents as Tokyo, Japan. In the Northeast and Southern California, some cities and their **suburbs** have grown so large that they are now "connected" in one large urban area, or **megalopolis**. In other parts of the United States, one can travel for many hours and never encounter a town with more than a few thousand inhabitants. Most of the major cities in the U.S. are located near sources of water or other natural resources.

Canada's population is more than 30 million. Almost two-thirds of the people in Canada live in the **provinces** of Ontario and Quebec. The country's largest cities are Toronto (2.5 million), Montreal (1.6 million), Calgary (1.0 million), Edmonton (700,000), and Vancouver (600,000). Only about 100,000 people live in Canada's three northern territories—Nunavut, Northwest Territory, and the Yukon. There are many parts of Canada that are still quite remote.

DOORWAY TO A NEW LIFE

The millions of immigrants that streamed into the United States and Canada from the mid-1800s to the mid-1900s did so by boat. Beginning in 1892, the major U.S. point of entry was Ellis Island in New York Harbor. More than 12 million people came through its doors. More than one-third of Americans can trace at least one ancestor back to Ellis Island. Canadian ports of entry included the cities of Quebec and Montreal in the east and Vancouver in the west. More than one million immigrants entered Canada through Pier 21 in Halifax, Nova Scotia. Both Ellis Island and Pier 21 are now national historic sites and museums.

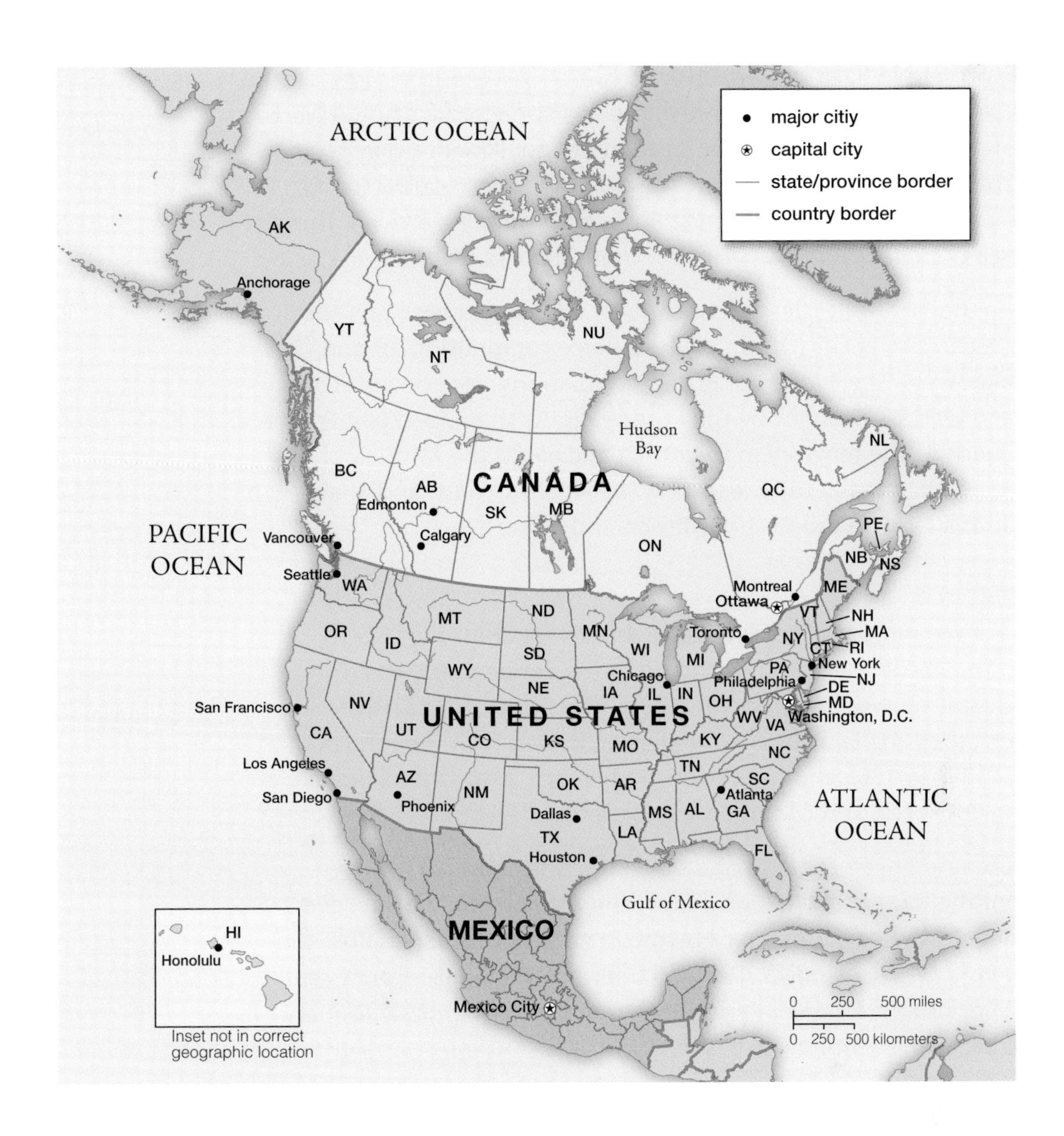

The United States and Canada are countries of both large cities and small towns. This map shows some of the major cities of both countries.

Population of the United States

1900	76,094,000 (does not include Alaska or Hawaii)
1950	152,271,417 (first census that includes both Alaska and Hawaii)
1990	249,464,396
2000	282,216,952
2007	301,139,947 (estimate)

Population of Canada

1901	5,371,000
1951	13,648,000
1991	28,031,000
2001	31,050,000
2007	33,390,141 (estimate)

Populating the U.S. and Canada

The first people to make the United States and Canada their home were groups of hunter-gatherers who **migrated** to North America over a land bridge from Asia. They were the ancestors of the people called Native Americans today. By the time the first European explorers arrived, these people had occupied North America for more than 12,000 years.

Starting in the 1600s, the desire to control the resources between the Atlantic Ocean and Pacific Ocean created fierce competition among European powers. The Native American populations were devastated by disease and warfare brought by the Europeans. By the mid-1700s, France claimed much of the territory in the north and along the Mississippi River. England had many **colonies** along the Atlantic coast, and Spain controlled the land on the Gulf of Mexico and in the West.

Independence

In 1754, France and Great Britain began a fight for control of North America. The battle that became known as the Seven Years War eventually spilled over to Europe and Asia. The fighting in North America is called the French and Indian War. Britain won the long and bloody conflict in 1763 and took control of French land east of the Mississippi River and French territory in Canada.

The thirteen American colonies had been asked to shoulder much of the cost of the long war with France, yet the colonists did not believe that their voices were being heard by the British government across the Atlantic. In 1776, the colonists declared their independence from Great Britain. They fought successfully for their freedom in the Revolutionary War and became the United States of America.

ALASKA

The largest U.S. state, Alaska, once belonged to Russia, which lies directly to the west. Secretary of State William Seward convinced the U.S. government to buy the territory in 1867 for two cents an acre. At the time, many Americans thought the purchase was a waste of money and called Alaska "Seward's Folly."

Yet Seward's decision proved to be a wise one. Alaska was soon found to have vast reserves of gold, oil, and other natural resources. It also became the center of the salmon industry. The Alaska Highway, which was built during the 1940s, enabled vehicles from Canada and the lower 48 states to reach the area. Alaska officially became the 49th state in 1959.

With the Louisiana Purchase from France in 1803, the U.S. doubled in size. Over the next few decades, the U.S. purchased Florida from Spain and bought or conquered the remaining land west of the Mississippi River from Britain and Mexico. By 1853, the map of the continental U.S. looked very much like it does today.

The Alaska Highway is about 1,500 miles (2,400 kilometers) long. It crosses some very remote areas of Canada and Alaska. Drivers have to watch out for animals that stray onto the road, such as caribou, moose, and sheep.

Meanwhile, present-day Canada remained under British control as a union of British colonies for many years. Canada would eventually gain its independence in a process that began in 1867.

According to legend, Canada got its name from the **Iroquois** word *Kannata*, which means "collection of huts." Explorer Jacques Cartier heard this word when speaking with two native boys and mistook it for the name of their land.

The origin of the name *America* is thought to come from the name of Amerigo Vespucci, the first European explorer to recognize that the continents of North and South America were not part of Asia but a separate landmass.

Natural Features

The landforms that make up the United States and Canada stretch across the countries' common border for more than 3,000 miles (4,800 kilometers). The western third contains great mountain ranges, including the Rocky Mountains. Like most mountain ranges in North America, the Rockies have a north-south orientation. They run from the Mexican border in the south to the western edge of Alaska in the north. Fruits and vegetables grow in great abundance in many of the valleys that lie between the mountains in the Rockies.

The middle third of the region consists of an enormous band of plains. The drier western edge of these plains is perfect for growing wheat and raising livestock; the wetter eastern edge produces corn, soybeans, and other important crops. The entire region is often called the Great Plains. It consists mostly of prairie land with tall grass and few trees. The term *prairie* comes from the French word for *meadow*. To the north of the Canadian prairie lies the Canadian Shield, a vast, rugged area of ancient rocks, where few people live.

The eastern third of the region consists of a coastal plain that begins at the Gulf of St. Lawrence and widens as it stretches south to the Gulf of Mexico. The St. Lawrence Lowlands, which lie to the west of the Laurentian Highlands (which are part of the Appalachian Mountains), are home to more than half of Canada's people.

← From the snow-covered land of Canada to the blazing sun of Arizona, the climate and physical geography of North America is as varied as its people. This is Lake Laberge, in the Yukon, Canada..

Because of its fertile land and many waterways, the eastern third of North America grew first and fastest—and still contains a large number of major cities. Much of the dividing line between Canada and the U.S. in the eastern part of the continent is formed by the Great Lakes.

ALL SHOOK UP

The west coast of North America is an active earthquake zone. There, several of the earth's **tectonic plates** collide. The San Andreas Fault is a well-known and closely monitored area where two plates meet. Sudden movement along the fault has caused two destructive earthquakes in the city of San Francisco—one in 1906 and another in 1989. Another fault, in the Mississippi River valley, is believed to have caused an extremely violent earthquake in the early 1800s. The earthquake actually changed the course of the river in some places.

Major bodies of water

Long before the United States and Canada even existed, the people who lived in this part of the world depended on oceans, lakes, and rivers for food, power, transportation, and protection. This is still true today.

With the exception of the U.S.-Mexican border, the United States and Canada are surrounded by water—the Pacific Ocean to the west, the Arctic Ocean to the north, the Atlantic Ocean to the east, and the Gulf of Mexico to the south. More than 1,000 miles (1,609 kilometers) of the border between the two countries is made up by the Great Lakes—Superior, Michigan, Huron, Erie, and Ontario—as well as the St. Lawrence River. The Great Lakes are the world's largest group of freshwater lakes.

In the days when the fastest way to travel was by boat, the oceans, lakes, and rivers of the region served as "highways" for transportation and business. For example, the chain of waterways formed by Lake Champlain, Lake George, and the Hudson River in New York state was once the fastest route from the Canadian cities of Montreal and Quebec to New York City.

The Great Lakes were the home of large naval and commercial vessels in the 1700s and 1800s. They still are very important shipping routes for the middle sections of the U.S. and Canada. Much of the region's iron ore, coal, and stone is transported via the Great Lakes. The lakes are also important sources of fish and drinking water. In recent years, the U.S. and Canadian governments have spent millions of dollars on finding ways to fight pollution to keep the water clean and safe.

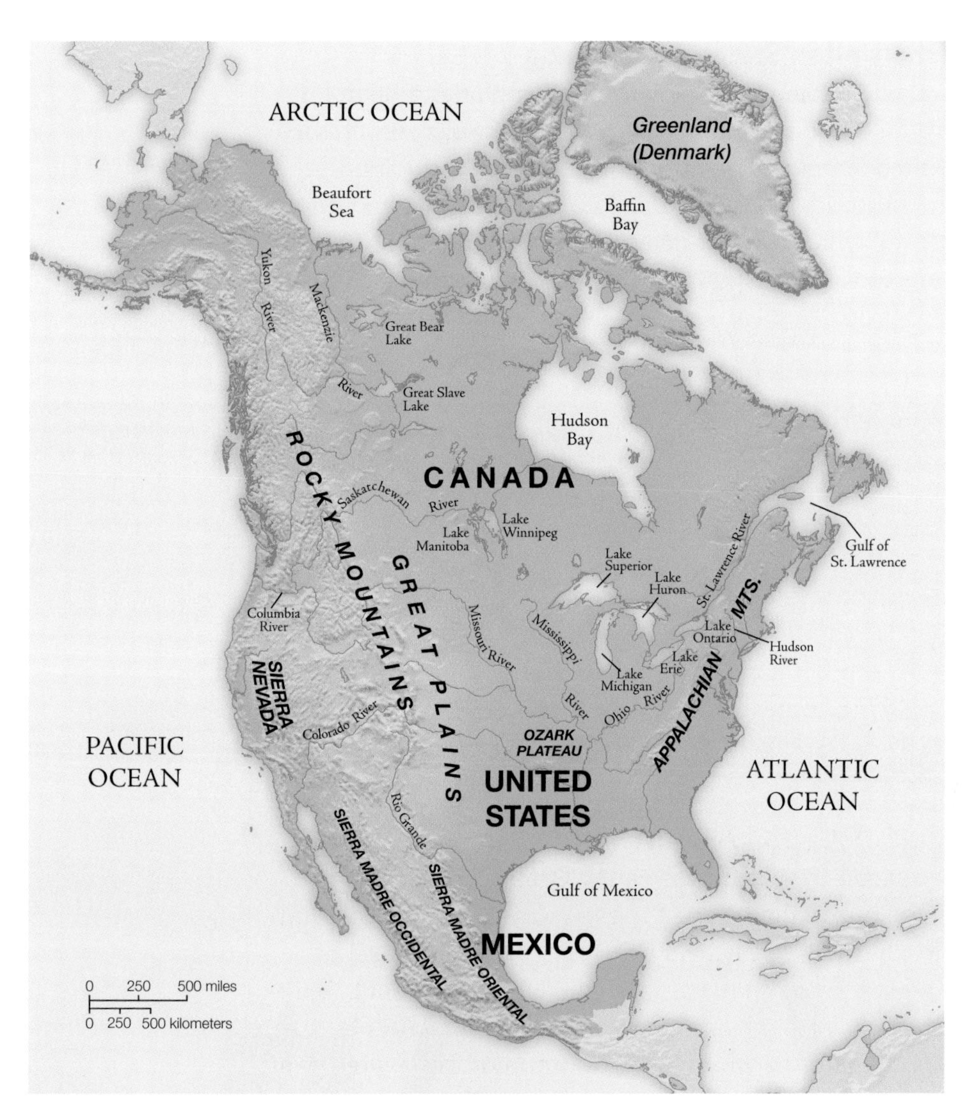

The rivers and waterways of North America helped exploration and trade in the region, while the mountain ranges were often obstacles that needed to be overcome.

FISH TALE

The rich waters off the eastern coast of Canada have been known to cod fisherman for at least 600 years. European fishing fleets visited this area frequently and may have been aware of the existence of North America many years before Christopher Columbus made his famous journey in 1492. The fishers were interested in new fishing grounds, not new continents, so their tales did not reach the ears of 15th-century explorers.

The rivers of the United States and Canada

Before the arrival of railroads, automobiles, and airplanes, the easiest way to move products and people was by water. In many cases, this is still true. The United States has many important rivers, including the Mississippi, Ohio, Missouri, Rio Grande, Colorado, Columbia, and Hudson. The Mississippi River, which flows from Minnesota to the Gulf of Mexico, is a lifeline for agriculture and industry. The Rio Grande forms part of the U.S. border with Mexico.

The Mississippi River holds an important place in American culture, history, and geography. The Gateway Arch in St. Louis, Missouri, is one of the most famous landmarks along the river.

Two of the most important rivers in Canada are the Mackenzie and the St. Lawrence. The Mackenzie starts in Great Slave Lake in central Canada and flows north to the Arctic Ocean. The St. Lawrence River connects the Atlantic Ocean to the Great Lakes. Through a system of locks and canals, called the St. Lawrence Seaway, large cargo ships can connect the "midsection" of North America to the rest of the world.

The St. Lawrence Seaway had begun as a dream 200 years prior to its completion in 1959. As the U.S. grew in the 1700s and 1800s, one of the country's major challenges was moving goods and people west. In 1825, a shipping canal was completed across New York State between Albany on the Hudson River, and Buffalo on Lake Erie. The Erie Canal stretched 363 miles (581 kilometers) and formed a connection between the interior section of North America and the Atlantic Ocean. The idea for such a canal was first proposed by English engineers a century earlier, but even they could not have foreseen its amazing impact. The cost of moving cargo west was reduced by more than 90 percent, which started a flood of goods and people across America.

Digging the canal required a tremendous workforce. Many of the workers on the Erie Canal were new immigrants from Ireland. They were the first of many waves of immigrants from across the Atlantic Ocean. The Erie Canal is now used only for recreational boating. Highways, railroad systems, and the St. Lawrence Seaway have taken its place.

Major Rivers in North America

River	Length in miles (kilometers)
Missouri	2,341 (3,767)
Mississippi	2,320 (3,733)
Yukon	2,300 (3,700)
Rio Grande	1,885 (3,034)
Colorado	1,450 (2,330)
Columbia	1,232 (1,982)
Mackenzie	1,079 (1,738)
Ohio	981 (1,579)
St. Lawrence	744 (1,197)
Hudson	315 (506)

Started in 1916, the Race to the Clouds is an annual auto race to the top of Pikes Peak in the Rocky Mountains of Colorado.

The mountains of the United States and Canada

There are two major mountainous regions in the United States and Canada. In the east, the Appalachian Mountains begin in Georgia and run north more than 1,500 miles (2,400 kilometers), reaching into southern Canada. The mountains continue on the other side of the St. Lawrence River as the Laurentian Highlands. Within the Appalachian Range are the Great Smoky Mountains, Pocono Mountains, Catskill Mountains, Green Mountains, and White Mountains. This mountain chain is an important natural resource for the people of the east. It provides water for **irrigation**, drinking, power, and transportation. The mountains are also a source of mineral wealth and lumber.

The Tallest Peaks in the United States and Canada

Mountain	State or Territory	Height in feet (meters)
Mount McKinley	Alaska	20,320 (6,194)
Mount Logan	Yukon Territory	19,550 (5,959)
Mount St. Elias	Alaska/Yukon Territory	18,008 (5,490)
Mount Foraker	Alaska	17,400 (5,303)
Mount Lucania	Yukon Territory	17,147 (5,226)

View from the top

In the west, the Rocky Mountains cover approximately 3,000 miles (4,800 kilometers) from the American Southwest up into western Canada. The Sierra Nevada, Cascades, Coast Mountains, and Alaska Range all run along the Pacific coast. The Brooks Range borders the Arctic Ocean in Alaska. All are considered part of the same major chain. As in the east, these mountain ranges provide water to the surrounding areas and are often rich in minerals. This has helped "mile-high cities" such as Denver and Calgary grow in size and importance.

Mountains are formed by the collision of tectonic plates. Plate movement can also trigger earthquakes and volcanic eruptions, both of which occur on the Pacific coast. In 1980, Mount St. Helens, a volcano in the Cascade Range in Washington State, erupted violently, causing great damage to people, property, and wildlife. Before the eruption, the mountain was more than 9,500 feet (2,900 meters) high. Today, it measures just 8,365 feet (2,550 meters) high.

Mount Rainier is an active volcano in Washington State. It is covered in snow and ice.

BIG WIND

One of the windiest places on Earth is Mount Washington, which is part of the White Mountains in New Hampshire. At 6,288 feet (1,918 meters), it is the tallest peak in the northeastern United States. A gust of 231 mph (372 kph), the strongest ever measured, was once recorded there.

The islands of the United States and Canada

Island living is not something most people picture when they think about life in the United States and Canada, but millions of people make islands their year-round homes. The most crowded is Manhattan Island, which is part of New York City. Staten Island, which forms part of New York Harbor, has about a half-million residents.

Across the water from Staten Island is Brooklyn, which is also part of New York City. Brooklyn is actually the western tip of another island, Long Island, which stretches east for 118 miles (190 kilometers). It is the largest island in the continental United States and also the most populated, with about 7.5 million people.

For those who prefer more privacy, there are plenty of quiet little islands—from the Pacific Northwest to the Thousand Islands in the St. Lawrence River—many of which are private islands with just one home.

Some of the most picturesque small towns in the United States are located on islands, including Nantucket and Martha's Vineyard off the coast of Massachusetts, and Key West at the tip of the Florida Keys.

Two of Canada's most beautiful islands are on opposite sides of the country. Located off the east coast, Prince Edward Island is the smallest of Canada's provinces and the most densely populated. A popular destination for tourists, Prince Edward Island is known for its lovely rolling hills and sand dunes.

ALOHA!

America's 50th state, Hawaii, is a group of 132 islands, with eight main islands—Hawaii, Kahoolawe, Kauai, Lanai, Maui, Molokai, Oahu and Niihau. The islands are actually made up of volcanoes that rose from the ocean floor. The Hawaiian Islands are the world's most remote island chain. They are about 2,400 miles (3,860 kilometers) from the California coast.

A ferry to Vancouver Island is used by both tourists and people commuting to and from the island for work.

Vancouver Island, the largest island on the west coast of Canada, is also a popular tourist spot. The island is named for George Vancouver, a British naval officer who explored the region in the 1790s. The city of Vancouver, which is on the Canadian mainland, is also named for him. The rivers and lakes of Vancouver Island are important fisheries for salmon and trout. The island's mountains are home to the greatest concentration of cougars in North America.

Ferry travel

Getting to and from the many islands in the United States and Canada would be almost impossible without the ferry service. Along the Alaskan coast, many towns are not easily reachable by car or plane. They depend on a ferry "highway" system. Ferries have been a vital part of the transportation system in North America for more than 250 years. In the days before large bridges were constructed, the best way for people and goods to cross rivers was by ferry. Today, many commuters take ferries to work. Ferry travel is a quick, relaxing way to avoid the bridge and tunnel traffic in busy cities, such as New York and Boston.

Climate of the United States and Canada

Because the United States and Canada cover such a vast area, the climate differs greatly across the region, depending on season and location. The northernmost reaches of Canada and Alaska are frozen **tundra**. At the southern part of the region, by contrast, Hawaii and South Florida are considered tropical. The tropics are defined as any place where the sun shines directly overhead during some part of the year. Tropical climates are typically warm and humid.

Subarctic conditions prevail in the area that extends from the Aleutian Islands in the west to Newfoundland in the east. This area is more than 1,000 miles (1,600 kilometers) wide in many places. Temperatures in the Aleutians are rarely extreme. However, this is one of the foggiest and rainiest places on Earth because cold air and moisture are always present. The conditions are similar in Newfoundland, but the weather there is harder to predict.

Much of the land in between the far western and eastern ends of the North American continent is part of the Canadian Shield. This vast area of ancient exposed bedrock is not good for farming and is extremely cold most of the year. The northern section is cold and desolate tundra.

Along the California coast, winters are generally mild and summers are hot and dry. Northwestern coastal areas get much more rain. The mountains and **deserts** of the west consist mostly of **arid** and semi-arid regions, which are dry much of the year. North America's largest deserts lie between the Rocky Mountains and the Sierra Nevada. The largest is the Great Basin Desert, which covers most of Nevada and parts of several other states. Located mostly in California, the Mojave Desert is famous for Death Valley, the lowest and hottest place in North America. Temperatures there often reach 120 °F (49 °C).

NATURE'S WRATH

Most scientists agree that humankind is affecting the world's climate and weather. They believe that **greenhouse gases** released by automobiles, factories, and other sources have helped to make the oceans warmer. This, in turn, has had a big impact on the weather. In August 2005, Hurricane Katrina entered the Gulf of Mexico. The warming of the water in the gulf caused Katrina to grow stronger as it approached Louisiana and Mississippi. When the hurricane struck land, it wiped out many coastal communities. The levees that protected the coastal city of New Orleans broke, and much of the city was flooded. More than 1,800 people lost their lives and rebuilding the area has cost tens of billions of dollars.

The rolling hills and tranquil land of Vermont form just one of the beautiful natural sites of North America. Vermont is sometimes known as a four-season state, because it has four distinct seasons. Its winters are cold, but its summers are usually mild.

The eastern half of the United States and Canada consists primarily of two climate regions. From central Texas across to the Middle Atlantic states, the climate is considered humid subtropical. Temperatures can range from 0 °F to 100 °F (–13 °C to 37 °C) during the year, with hot, humid summers and plenty of precipitation year-round. From the Interior Plains of Canada, through the Great Lakes region, and east to New England and Nova Scotia, the climate is cooler and somewhat drier. This type of climate is known as humid continental.

Fall colors

One of the most popular attractions in the U.S. and Canada is the changing of the leaves each fall. Many people take vacations to see the fall colors, particularly in eastern Canada and New England. The climate in southern Canada and much of the U.S. supports **deciduous forests**. In fall, the leaves on deciduous trees turn from green to various shades or red, yellow, orange, and brown before they drop to the ground.

People

Only a small percentage of the people living in the United States and Canada can claim to be descendants of the **indigenous** people who came to the continent from Asia more than 12,000 years ago. The vast majority of Canadians and Americans trace their roots to immigrants who came by ship or later by airplane. What brought many immigrants to the region—and still does—is a combination of pushing and pulling forces.

As populations grew in Europe, Asia, Africa, South America, Central America, and the Caribbean, land and jobs became more scarce. In many cases, people from these regions were denied their basic freedoms and human rights. They were not necessarily forced from their homelands, but they believed a better life awaited them elsewhere. Desperate for new opportunities, they risked everything to come to the United States and Canada. More often than not, they found the opportunities they sought and put down roots.

The combined population of the United States and Canada is expected to climb above 400 million within a few generations. Even so, both countries are still viewed as places where a person who works hard can find open doors and open space. Immigrants have made the United States and Canada dynamic and diverse nations. Each wave of newcomers poses challenges to society and faces daunting obstacles. However, in the history of these countries, society has become stronger because of the contributions of immigrants.

← Colorado is one of the places where suburban development is increasing.

African Americans

African slaves are the only major immigrant group that came to North America against their will. Slavery was legal in most of the United States until the early 1800s and in the Southern states until the mid-1860s. Canada offered slaves freedom, and many thousands escaped over the border through a system of safe houses called the Underground Railroad. From 1914 to 1950, millions of African Americans migrated to major northern cities, looking for better economic opportunities and a relief from racial discrimination. This movement is known as the Great Migration. The Harlem Renaissance, a major movement in U.S. art and culture, is a direct result of the Great Migration. In the 1980s, many African Americans (and other Americans) began moving to southern cities, such as Atlanta, Georgia. Like the Great Migration, this movement was primarily a search for better economic opportunities. The issue of race and racism is an ongoing discussion throughout the United States.

NEW HOMES AWAY FROM HOME

About 1.5 million immigrants enter the United States each year. Traditionally, most immigrants have settled in the states of New York, New Jersey, Florida, Illinois, Texas, and California. Since 2000, however, North Carolina, South Carolina, Alabama, Indiana, Wisconsin, and Colorado have been receiving immigrants at triple their previous rate.

Indigenous people

When Europeans first arrived in present-day Canada and the United States, the people they met had been living on the land for thousands of years. The native inhabitants had complex cultures and sophisticated belief systems. Most viewed their land as a living thing that no one could own. By contrast, the settlers came from societies in which land was the most precious thing one could possess.

Almost immediately, the newcomers started acquiring tribal land. Sometimes they bought or traded for it, and sometimes they just took it. Many **treaties** were made and then quickly broken. When the native people resisted, wars broke out, which led to the loss of even more land. In 1830, the United States passed a law that forced the native people of the east to move west of the Mississippi. Eventually, almost all of the major tribes were pushed onto government reservations. Many tribes people were denied citizenship for generations.

Both the United States and Canada have taken measures in recent years to restore some of the rights and property taken from indigenous people. Many religious and cultural artifacts in museums have been returned to their original peoples, and ancient human remains have been given proper burial. There is controversy surrounding some returned objects, however. For example, who has the right to the human remains that are older than any known Native American tribes?

WHAT'S IN A NAME?

Christopher Columbus referred to the people he came across as Indians, because he believed he had landed in India. Today, people have different opinions as to what is the most accurate and respectful term for such people. The most common terms are *Native American* and *American Indian*. Canadians often use the term *First Nations* to describe indigenous people.

The United States has hundreds of Indian reservations, both large and small. Canada has more than 600 Indian reserves. This one is in the Yukon..

This Catholic wedding is taking place in Quebec, Canada. In the United States and Canada, people are free to have ceremonies of any religion.

Religion in the United States and Canada

Both the United States and Canada guarantee religious freedom to their people and offer legal protection to those who are victimized because of their faith. In fact, both nations have special laws that fight religious hate crimes with especially harsh punishment. For four centuries, people have come to this part of the world to escape religious **persecution** in their own countries. At the same time, religious freedom in the United States and Canada has enabled immigrants to transplant their faith and preserve a precious part of their old culture.

Religious freedom was particularly important to the American colonists in the 1700s. They wanted to keep religion out of government, so that no church would gain too much power. This separation of church and state became an important part of the U.S. Constitution. Keeping the two separate is not always easy. The U.S. and Canada, for example, encourage religion through their support of certain charities and by giving tax breaks to religious institutions. Also, in some cases, a person's religious beliefs or practices may conflict with the law. For example, Christian Scientists do not believe in seeking medical care. In some U.S. states, parents have been taken to court for refusing to give their children medical care that conflicts with their religious beliefs.

Today, virtually every religion in the world is practiced in the United States and Canada. About two out of three people in these countries describe themselves as religious or "somewhat" religious. The largest religion is Christianity, but **Judaism**, **Islam**, **Buddhism**, and **Hinduism** all have a million or more followers.

Religion and church remain an important part of U.S. culture, especially in the southern states. This service is taking place in a Baptist church in Alabama.

Religious groups

United States

Religious Group	Approximate Number of Followers
Non-Catholic Christian	108.7 million
Roman Catholic	50.8 million
Jewish	2.8 million
Muslim	1.1 million
Buddhist	1.1 million
Hindu	800,000

Canada

Religious Group	Approximate Number of Followers
Roman Catholic	12.9 million
Non-Catholic Christian	8.7 million
Muslim	600,000
Jewish	300,000
Buddhist	300,000
Hindu	300,000
Sikh	300,000

Government in the United States

The United States was a brave experiment in **democracy**. In 1776, a group of colonial leaders signed the Declaration of Independence, knowing that if their plan failed it would likely cost them their lives. They risked everything to win their freedom from Great Britain and asked their fellow colonists to do the same. The British were very good at fighting against armies and navies, but they were unable to defeat an "idea." The colonists won their independence and created a federal republic that still exists today.

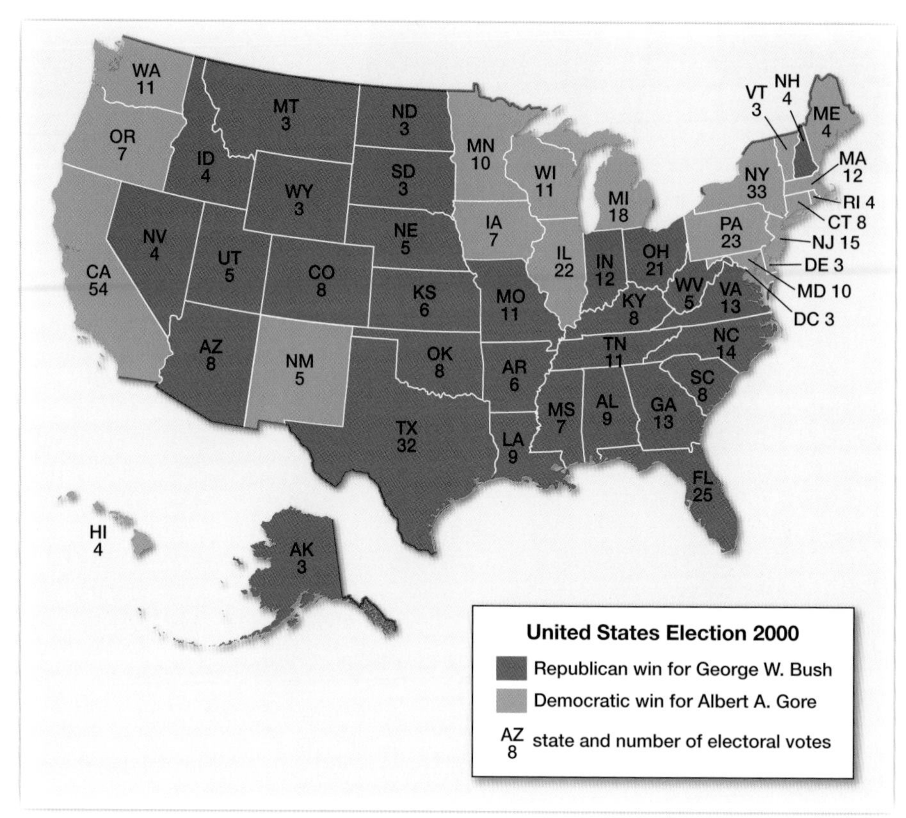

In the United States, the presidential election is not decided by the total number of votes cast for each candidate. Instead, the candidate who receives the most votes in each state earns a number of electoral votes that reflect that state's population. In the 2000 election, Democrat Al Gore received more total votes than his Republican opponent, George W. Bush. However, as this map illustrates, Bush (red states) finished with more electoral votes than Gore (blue states) and was elected president.

Every four years, the people of the United States vote for a president, who functions as the country's chief executive. A president may only serve two four-year terms. The president's powers are shared with the Senate, which is made up of 100 senators (two from each state), and the House of Representatives, which has more than 400 representatives. Together, the two bodies are known as Congress. Congress writes the nation's laws, directs its **domestic** and foreign policies, and decides how the taxes collected from the people should be spent.
The Supreme Court is the third branch of the government.

It consists of nine justices, who decide court cases that involve either international issues or Constitutional issues. The three-branch system of government provides the U.S. with checks and balances to make sure that no single individual or group abuses its power. If the people are unhappy with the government, they have the means to change it through their votes.

Government in Canada

Canada is a federation of ten provinces and three territories. A part of the British Empire from 1763, Canada gained the right to self-government in 1849 and became a **dominion** in 1867. In 1931, Canada was declared a "partner nation" by Britain—equal in status but loyal to Britain's royal family. In 1982, Queen Elizabeth II signed the Constitution Act, which cut the last legal ties between Canada and Britain. Though independent, Canada remains part of the Commonwealth, and Elizabeth II continues to be Canada's queen.

In Canada, whichever party has the most votes gets to choose the prime minister. Here, Prime Minister Justin Trudeau speaks to his supporters in 2015.

Canadians elect representatives to serve in the House of Commons, where important issues are debated and laws are created. There are more than 300 elected officials in the House of Commons, each of whom represents a district within Canada. This is where the power lies in Canada's political system. The governor general is the official representative of the queen and therefore Canada's leading political figure. However, the country is actually run by the prime minister, who is the head of the political party that receives the most votes. The prime minister works with the governor general to appoint members of the country's Senate. The Senate and House of Commons make up Canada's Parliament. Both bodies must approve new laws, but the Senate rarely blocks the laws passed by the House of Commons.

WOMEN IN POWER

In 1993, Canada's Progressive Conservative Party named Defense Minister Kim Campbell the country's prime minister. It marked the first time a woman had led Canada's government. Campbell served only four months before her party lost its majority in national elections. Campbell's brief term was the crowning achievement in a career that also saw her become the first woman to serve as Canada's minister of justice, **attorney general**, and head of its Progressive Conservative Party.

The U.S. has had many women in influential positions, but has never had a female head of state.

Condoleezza Rice was the second woman to become U.S. secretary of state. The secretary of state is the president's top adviser on U.S. foreign policy. →

IN SICKNESS AND IN HEALTH?

One of the most complex issues facing the United States and Canada is the availability of quality health care and what role the government should play in making sure its citizens receive proper medical care. In Canada, the government guarantees all permanent citizens free health care, regardless of their income. Each province and territory runs its own health-care system. Many Canadians complain that they must wait too long to see doctors and that medical technology and equipment are not up-to-date.

In the U.S., the government provides health care only for the elderly, poor, and disabled. Everyone else must either have health insurance through their jobs or pay for care themselves. Millions of Americans, including more than 10 million children, cannot afford health insurance or proper health care. In a country with the best doctors and best medical technology, these people have almost no access to modern medicine.

Some Americans try to take advantage of Canada's cheaper medicines by traveling across the border to purchase large quantities or by buying them through the mail. The laws are unclear as to whether this practice is allowed. Legal or not, it is a sign that the current system needs improvement.

City life

Most of the major cities in the United States and Canada sprung up in areas that are either close to agriculture or natural resources or that are convenient places to store and ship goods. Such areas serve as central locations where goods can be bought, sold, warehoused, processed, and sent to other places.

Eastern cities such as Boston, Philadelphia, Baltimore, and Charleston, South Carolina, grew large and rich because they were busy natural ports. New York City became especially powerful because it also linked to the Hudson River, which was a gateway to the American West in the early 1800s.

With the coming of the railroads in the 1800s, cities such as Chicago, Kansas City, and Dallas grew quickly in the middle of America. Shipping across the Great Lakes helped industrial cities, such as Toronto and Detroit, flourish. Cities such as Montreal, New Orleans, and St. Louis benefited from their proximity to large rivers.

Cities in the west formed in similar ways. A gold strike in California turned San Francisco into a major city almost overnight. Gold also drew people to Vancouver, which later became Canada's major western port and also an important city in the lumber business.

These children may have different ethnic backgrounds, but they are all clearly Americans.

Population shift

As more jobs awaited workers in city offices and factories—and improved farming techniques produced more food on less land—populations began to shift from rural farm areas to urban city areas. Over the past century, the number of people living in agricultural areas has shrunk dramatically, while the populations in cities in the United States and Canada have exploded.

As cities became more crowded, some city dwellers began to move to suburbs (see photo on page 22). In recent years, the suburbs around many cities have become so crowded that people are moving even farther away, to communities called exurbs.

Today, many of the people pouring into suburbs are immigrants. Typically, newcomers to the United States and Canada make their homes in cities, where they are likely to find neighborhoods where others from their country live. Making a new life in a strange land is much easier when the language, food, and customs are familiar. In some cities, more than 100 different languages can be heard. However, as housing prices have risen in many cities, more and more immigrants are settling outside the traditional urban areas.

Suburban poverty

Many people who move from cities to suburbs believe that they are escaping poverty and the problems it creates. In one way, they are correct—the poverty rate in cities is higher than in the suburbs. However, there are now more people living in poverty in the suburbs than in the cities. A major reason for this change is that immigrants—who fill many low-paying jobs—are bypassing traditional urban neighborhoods and moving directly to the suburbs.

For some people, nothing can take the place of the excitement of living in a big city, such as New York.

Culture

Rapid change is part of life for the people who call the United States or Canada home. Popular culture is constantly blending old traditions with new trends. This affects the way people eat, dress, live, and communicate. Sometimes change is for the better, and sometimes it is for the worse. But everyone wants to know: "What's the next big thing?"

The U.S. and Canada have traditionally opened their arms to people from all over the world. Historically, the two nations have embraced newcomers in different ways. *Melting Pot* is a term that describes the approach to immigration in the U.S. for most of its history. The term meant that immigrants were expected to blend their cultures into the larger culture of the country. This common goal gave the country great strength and diversity, and a tremendous amount of national pride.

In recent years, there has been less "melting" and more "combining" of ingredients. Being an American no longer means being the same as everyone else. Cultural differences that once were met with fear or intolerance are now being celebrated for the diversity they bring to American culture. For example, the influence of cultures from Mexico, Central and South America, and the Caribbean has changed the way the country looks, sounds, and tastes—all in less than a generation.

← For generations of immigrants, the Statue of Liberty in New York was the first welcoming sight of their new home.

Cultural blends in Canada

Canada has long encouraged its many **ethnic groups** to preserve their cultural identity, and in some cases, this right is protected by law. The French-speaking people of Quebec, for example, trace their roots back more than 400 years. The Canadian government has recognized Quebeckers as being members of a distinct society. In the Canadian Plains, other European cultures are recognized and celebrated in cities such as Saskatoon and Regina.

The Canadian government gave the Inuit people their own national homeland, Nunavut, where they live and work in ways that help maintain their cultural heritage. In Canada, it is not unusual for official notices to be translated into several languages.

THE FRENCH IN QUEBEC

When England gained control over Canada in the 1700s, most of its citizens spoke French. Today, English is spoken throughout the country, but French-speaking people still make up the majority in Quebec. For many years, they faced prejudice and were denied opportunities because they did not speak English. In the 1960s, they began fighting for their rights, and in 1976 they won control of the provincial government. Since then, many Quebeckers have tried to make Quebec a separate country.

Immigration

The first North American settlers were English, Dutch, French, and German. They were followed in the 1800s and early 1900s by millions of immigrants from Ireland, Italy, Scandinavia, and Eastern Europe. Over the past century, the number of people from Asia, Africa, and South and Central America has increased dramatically. Each group has brought important skills that helped make their new countries stronger, as well as new ideas in music, food, and art that have further enriched the quality of life. Today, the sights, sounds, tastes, and even the technologies—from small towns to big cities—are greatly influenced by ideas that came from other parts of the world.

The United States and Canada have strict laws for people from other countries who wish to become citizens. Not everyone follows these laws, however. Some people who face economic hardship, war, or political injustice in their homeland are unwilling to undergo the official immigration process and choose instead to live in the U.S. and

The issue of how to deal with immigrants who come to the U.S. illegally is an ongoing, heated debate. This is a border patrol on the border of California and Mexico.

Canada illegally. The United States accepts about one million legal immigrants each year (more than all other countries combined), but about another 700,000 immigrants come without permission. More than half of all illegal immigrants come across the United States' 2,000-mile (3,220-kilometer) border with Mexico. Most of the illegal immigrants in Canada are visitors who choose not to leave after their two-year visas expire or who apply for but fail to get refugee status. In 1986, Canada gave amnesty to its illegal immigrants. Since then, an estimated 200,000-plus illegal immigrants have come to Canada.

COUNTRIES OF ORIGIN

People from all over the world come to settle in the United States and Canada. These pie charts show the country of birth of each nation's population.

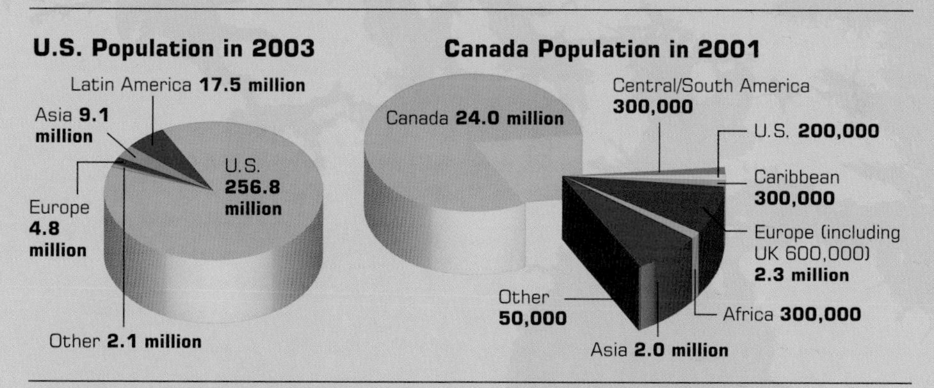

Beginning in the 1840s, a large wave of immigrants from Ireland arrived in the United States and Canada. They left their homeland because the potato crop suffered a blight, and millions of people were starving. Irish immigrants provided much of the muscle needed to build railroads, canals, and cities, and became a major force in American business, politics, and religion.

Entertainment and the arts in the United States and Canada

The role played by art and entertainment in the relationship between the United States and Canada is a long and complicated one. Because there is no language barrier between the two countries, a great deal of the television shows and movies enjoyed by Canadians originate from New York and Hollywood. However, many Canadians believe that the United States has too much influence on their culture. The Canadian government supports efforts to promote Canadian artists and entertainers, and to showcase their work as much as possible.

In the U.S., outside influences always seem to be welcome, particularly in music. Three of the world's most popular forms of music—jazz, rock, and the blues—all originated in the United States. Each musical style has its roots in Africa. Blues music evolved from the work songs sung by slaves and often features a "call and response" pattern that dates back

Each year, the city of Montreal hosts the largest jazz festival in the world.

to their African homelands. Jazz developed in New Orleans, where the percussion and rhythm of African music mixed with European chords and instrumentation. Rock was a combination of many musical styles, including the blues and gospel music from African-American churches. More recent American musical genres, such as rhythm and blues and rap, are heavily influenced by these earlier styles.

HOLLYWOOD'S CANADIAN CONNECTION

In early days of movie-making, most movies were shot on stages in Hollywood. Later, more movies were shot "on location" in various cities and countries around the world. Today, many movies whose stories take place in the U.S. are actually filmed in Canada, particularly in Vancouver and Toronto. The laws in Canada make filming there much less expensive.

The 2004 movie *Mean Girls* was filmed in Canada, although the story is set in the U.S.

Many communities celebrate their diversity by holding festivals featuring foods of different areas. At this Asian culture festival in Florida, Thai women are offering Thai food.

Food

One of the best ways to learn about a country is to enjoy its national dish. In the United States and Canada, this is easier said than done. The food in these countries is influenced by people with ties to more than 200 different nations. In general, most families try to sit down to a meal that includes some sort of meat, a vegetable, and a starch, such as bread, pasta, or rice. Often these ingredients are combined in one dish. Most meals also include a sweet dessert. Because of the availability of so many foods in the U.S. and Canada, and their relatively low cost, a family can vary its menu greatly from day to day.

Of all the foods popular in Canada, the one that is available almost everywhere is poutine. Poutine is made of fried potatoes mixed with curd cheese and smothered in gravy. It can be a messy dish, but few foods do a better job warming you up on a cold day. Canada's most famous food product is maple syrup. In fact, the maple leaf is one of the country's national symbols.

The United States does not have anything like a national dish. However, the favorite American foods have one thing in common: they can be eaten on the go. In the 1800s, visitors to the U.S. often remarked how quickly people sat down and ate their meals. In the 1900s, Americans began eating foods that did not even require them to sit down, such hamburgers, hot dogs, and ice-cream cones. These three foods gained nationwide popularity in 1904 at the World's Fair in St. Louis and are still among America's favorites today. The traditional food for which the U.S. is best known is probably turkey, which is the centerpiece of the Thanksgiving meal.

The many types of ethnic foods and flavors available in the United States and Canada provide adventurous cooks with an almost limitless number of taste combinations. Combining foods from two or more cultures is known as fusion cooking. Today, restaurants and cookbooks offering this kind of cross-over cuisine are extremely popular.

Supersized

One of the greatest challenges facing the United States and Canada in the 21st century is the problem of obesity. The foods that are easiest to buy and simplest to prepare tend to be highly processed and full of salt and fat. In the past, many people worked in jobs that involved physical activity, such as in factories or on farms. Today, many people work more sedentary desk jobs. In some neighborhoods, it is not considered safe for kids to play outside, and many schools no longer offer recess or gym as part of the day's activities. These factors mean that Americans and Canadians get far less physical activity than in the past. Today, one in six Canadians is considered to be obese. In the U.S., the number is closer to one in five. Obesity can lead to other health problems, such as diabetes, high blood pressure, and heart disease. This trend toward obesity may place a great burden on the health-care systems of both countries.

Different regions of the U.S. enjoy different food specialties. For example, lobster is a prized delicacy along the eastern seaboard.

Sports in the United States and Canada

In both Canada and the United States, sports are seen as an essential part of daily life and as a key part of a child's education. Sports are thought to teach important skills, such as leadership and cooperation. Sports stars are highly regarded and well paid, and often become role models for children and teens. For children in poor rural and urban areas, doing well in sports can be seen as a ticket out of their current situation and into college or a successful professional career.

The Olympic Games are popular viewing in both the United States and Canada. At the 2004 Games in Athens, Greece, U.S. sprinter Justin Gatlin won the gold medal in the final of the men's 100 meters and celebrated his victory with his fans.

IT CAME FROM CANADA

Three of the most popular sports in the U.S. have their roots in Canada. Ice hockey was played by British soldiers stationed in Canada in the 1850s. They combined a game they had seen in other parts of the empire with a game played by the indigenous people on the ice. Basketball was first conceived in Massachusetts in 1892 by James Naismith, a Canadian-born teacher who had been an outstanding athlete at McGill University in Montreal. McGill students also greatly influenced football. In 1874, they played two games against Harvard—one with McGill rules and one with Harvard rules. The Harvard players decided to adopt McGill's style, and this is the game that spread throughout the U.S.

In the United States, the most popular team sports are basketball, soccer, football, baseball, and softball. In Canada, ice hockey and lacrosse are regarded as the national sports. Tennis and golf are among the most popular individual sports. In recent years, more and more athletes have embraced the challenges of nature. Hunting and fishing have always been extremely popular, particularly in Canada, but now "outdoor sports"—including rock climbing, snowboarding, mountain biking, and kayaking—are attracting millions of new participants each year.

Many of the sports that started in the U.S. and Canada have become very popular in other parts of the world, particularly basketball. Baseball and ice hockey are also being played elsewhere in the world. The world's most popular sport, soccer, is popular among young Americans and Canadians but has yet to catch on as a major spectator sport.

WHAT ARE YOU WATCHING?

Top Spectator Sports in Canada

1. Ice Hockey
2. Lacrosse
3. Curling
4. Canadian Football

Top Spectator Sports in the U.S.

1. Pro Football
2. Baseball
3. College Football
4. Motor Sports (such as NASCAR)

CENTENARIO GR

Natural Resources and Economy

From the time the first European settlers arrived in the New World, they knew it was a land of almost limitless natural resources. Over the next five centuries, the abundance of resources the land had to offer would surpass even their wildest dreams. The soil was fertile and water was plentiful, and thick forests and mineral deposits covered millions of square miles. In their rush to **exploit** these resources, Americans and Canadians did not always protect the environment. Pollution and contamination of water, air, and soil have become controversial issues in both countries.

The United States is the world's second-largest producer of fossil fuels, which include petroleum, coal, and natural gas. The most abundant areas for oil and gas are in Alaska and the Gulf of Mexico. There are also vast coal deposits in and around the Appalachian Mountains. Canada also produces large amounts of oil and gas, mostly in the provinces of Alberta, Saskatchewan, and Manitoba. America's mineral wealth includes copper, gold, iron ore, and lead. Much of Canada's mining industry is concentrated in and around the Canadian Shield. More than 80 percent of its iron ore comes from the region where Quebec and Newfoundland meet.

← Both the U.S. and Canada have a great dependence on fuel. This oil rig is drilling in the Gulf of Mexico.

Protecting the environment

The need for fuel energy in the United States and Canada has led to oil and gas drilling in environmentally sensitive areas. The two governments must weigh the needs of their people against the damage these activities do to land, water, and animals. In 1989, one of the largest oil spills ever occurred in Prince William Sound in Alaska, devastating the environment.

ORE LINK

The industrial partnership between the United States and Canada first flourished in the late 1800s. The iron ore mined in Canada was carried via the Great Lakes to steel mills in Pennsylvania and Ohio, which were powered by coal mined in the Appalachian Mountains. This partnership helped the two economies to soar.

Agriculture in the United States and Canada

The U.S. has many millions of acres of extremely fertile soil. The rich, dark earth found in parts of the Southeast and Midwest is considered to be among the best in the world. Along the Mississippi and other major rivers in the country's midsection, the soil deposited by floods is also very good for farming. In the warm, humid mountain valleys along the Pacific coast, fruits and vegetables can be grown all year long.

American farmers grow enough food each year to feed the entire country, with plenty left over to send to other hungry people around the world. The yield per acre of American farms has been steadily rising, as new techniques for planting and harvesting crops have been introduced. One change that has people worried, however, is genetic modifications that have been introduced to crops such as soybeans. These modifications are done to make crops more resistant to diseases, insects, and bad weather. Although American farmers insist that the changes they have made are safe, many countries in Europe and Asia disagree. They have moved to ban the import of products made with genetically modified foods. Some countries in Africa refuse to take donations of genetically modified crops.

Most of Canada's agricultural production takes place in the central provinces, where vast wheat fields and gigantic cattle herds cover the landscape. The Laurentian Lowlands are home to hundreds of fruit, vegetable, and dairy farms. In all, a little more than 10 percent of Canada's land is useful for farming, but nearly half is covered by forest. This has made the country one of the world's largest lumber producers.

CANADA'S BREADBASKET

The wheat fields of Canada's Alberta province not only put bread on the table for almost every Canadian, they also feed the world. Much of the grain harvested in Alberta is transported to the coast of British Columbia, where it is shipped all over the **Pacific Rim**. Canada is second only to the United States in grain exports. The wheat fields of Alberta make up the northern part of a great fertile plain that stretches south to the Gulf of Mexico.

Techniques for harvesting wheat have changed over the years, but the United States and Canada still provide much of the wheat used around the world.

A worker in the aerospace industry examines the hydraulic pipes on a piece of equipment.

Business in the United States and Canada

The natural resources of the United States and Canada made both countries rich and powerful in the 19th and 20th centuries. The steel, lumber, mining, and manufacturing businesses provided work for millions of people and helped support railroads, shipbuilding, and other heavy industry. In recent times, competition from other parts of the world has reduced the importance of these "old" industries.

With a large, skilled workforce from which to draw, American and Canadian companies in "new" industries have begun to thrive. These industries include aerospace, information technology, pharmaceutical research, education, and communications. The fastest-growing job market in the United States and Canada is in **service industries**. Service industry jobs are as different as waiter, hotel manager, and lawyer.

As opportunities expand for people trained in the service and professional industries, the job market for many others is shrinking. Those with experience in traditional business such as manufacturing sometimes find that their talents are no longer needed. Thanks to new technologies, the hands-on work once performed by many are now being performed by few. The jobs they used to perform are now being done for less money by laborers in foreign countries.

Companies in a wide range of industries are **outsourcing**, or finding sources of labor outside the U.S. and Canada. Most simple manufacturing jobs are now done by low-paid workers, often women and children, in developing nations. Some dangerous jobs are also outsourced, because safety standards in the U.S. and Canada are high, which adds to the cost of the final product.

GOING GREEN

Environmental damage is not only caused by big, "dirty" industries. Every company in the United States and Canada has contributed to the pollution problem in some way, often without realizing it. After years of looking the other way, businesses are now looking for ideas that will help minimize their impact on the environment. Factories are "scrubbing" their emissions and disposing of their waste products more carefully, and smaller businesses are "going green"—finding small ways they can save energy, reduce waste, and encourage **sustainability**.

Advances in telecommunications have also led to outsourcing. Today, many U.S. and Canadian companies hire operators and telephone representatives who live and work in South Asia, where English is typically spoken as a second language. The cost of living in these countries is much lower than in the U.S. and Canada, so companies are able to pay workers much lower wages. Many people in the U.S. and Canada are opposed to outsourcing because it takes jobs from workers in their countries. Others argue that outsourcing helps the economy by keeping production costs down.

Older workers

People in the U.S. and Canada are living and working longer than ever before. Businesses are beginning to realize that the experience older workers bring to a job can be a great advantage, and many companies are starting programs that enable employees in their 60s and 70s to work part-time. As older people make up a greater percentage of the population, businesses that cater to their special needs are expected to experience rapid growth. As a result, many of today's young people will one day find themselves working in jobs related to health care and physical therapy.

Making a living in the United States and Canada

For many generations, newcomers to the U.S. and Canada have typically filled the hardest, lowest-paying jobs. They hoped that their children and grandchildren would build on this foundation and make better lives for themselves. Immigrants often faced racial and cultural barriers, but thanks to large public education systems and growing economies, the dreams of immigrant families were often fulfilled.

Today, more than half of American workers are professionals (such as doctors, teachers, or scientists), managers (such as business executives), or are involved in sales, office administration, or a technical job. In Canada, the percentage is even higher.

One key to the success of working people in the U.S. and Canada has been mobility. With so many places to live and work, most people can move quite easily if promising opportunities arise elsewhere. This has led to the breakup of long-established ethnic neighborhoods and to the spreading out of families. However, with transportation and communication being inexpensive and reliable, vast distances seem to get "closer" by the day.

Will the employment picture continue to change at this rapid pace? Most experts don't believe so. When today's schoolchildren begin their working careers, the job picture will probably look similar to what it is today. The greatest growth will still come in the professional and service sectors, as well as in business and finance. The number of construction, transportation, maintenance, and repair jobs will also grow.

Education will be an important part of job growth. In recent years, the United States and Canada have relied on people in other countries to perform some jobs related to science and technology. Educators are hoping to change this trend, with the help of government-sponsored programs that nurture interest in math and science among students.

UNDOCUMENTED WORKERS

For an economy to thrive, it must have people willing to do the hard, dirty, and sometimes dangerous jobs that require unskilled manual labor. The hours are long and the pay is often low. In the U.S. and Canada, these jobs have become very difficult to fill. Often, the jobs are taken by people who are living in these countries illegally. Because they are undocumented workers, their employment choices are very limited.

This practice has caused tremendous controversy. Those who say illegal workers should be deported from the country admit that there is no one else to fill these crucial jobs. Those who recognize the importance of these workers fear the impact on the economy if they were all granted citizenship. The workers themselves believe that their contributions to American and Canadian society deserve recognition—if not through citizenship, then through improved working conditions, expanded legal rights, and better pay.

During a 2003 power blackout, workers of all types made their way over the Brooklyn Bridge in New York. The United States and Canada need workers with a variety of skills and talents.

Transportation and communication

For industrial powers like the United States and Canada, the movement of people, products, raw materials, and ideas is critically important. Until the mid-1800s, nothing traveled faster than a boat or horse could carry it. The telegraph and railroad changed life on the North American continent dramatically. A telegraph link to Europe was established in 1866 and more than 200,000 miles (322,000 kilometers) of telegraph wire had been installed in the U.S. and Canada by the end of the decade.

The freeway system in Los Angeles is one of the busiest and most complex in the world.

The first cross-country rail line in the U.S. was completed in 1869. The Canadian Pacific Railway was finished in 1885. Wherever a railroad line existed, a telegraph wire was constructed, as well. By the end of the 1800s, almost anyone in the two countries could communicate or do business with anyone else, no matter where they were located.

With the arrival of the automobile in the 20th century, major cities in the United States and Canada were soon linked by paved roads and later by modern highways. With air travel, a journey that once took weeks now took hours. Today, the Internet enables people all over the United States and Canada—and the world—to exchange ideas, goods, and money in the blink of an eye.

WORKING ONLINE

As energy becomes more expensive and time becomes more precious, more and more businesses and government agencies in the United States and Canada are trying to overcome the challenges of geography by relying on the Internet. Doing work or attending classes from home via computer—sometimes called telecommuting—is starting to become a popular alternative. Telecommuting keeps people out of their cars and gives them more control over how they spend their time. It is also an excellent option for some parents who want to work and spend time with their children.

Telecommuting also lowers operating costs for many businesses, because they can have more workers in smaller office spaces. On the other hand, because workers can live farther away from work, telecommuting may contribute to the problem of urban sprawl. Telecommuting can also prevent people from forming close relationships and communities with their coworkers, adding to a sense of isolation that many people feel.

← A 2006 study showed that only 23 percent of U.S. workers have the option to work from home, but 59 percent of all workers would like to work from home at least some of the time. Thirty-eight percent wanted to work both in an office and from home, and 21 percent would prefer to work from home full-time.

ASIAN CONNECTION

The fastest-growing markets for many goods produced in the United States and Canada are in Asia. That makes British Columbia and the Pacific Northwest in the U.S. important regions. Already, cities such as Vancouver and Seattle have become "international" cities. In the 1990s, before the British colony of Hong Kong was handed over to the People's Republic of China, thousands of businesspeople and their families left Hong Kong for the west coast of North America. These people continued to do business with their Pacific Rim trading partners.

Immigrants from other Asian countries have also relocated to the U.S. and Canada. Many coastal cities now have large populations of Chinese, Japanese, and Koreans. The change is especially noticeable in British Columbia, where an estimated one in ten people speaks an Asian language fluently.

The future

In many parts of the world, neighboring countries focus on the things that divide them. However, the United States and Canada understand that they are partners that must work together to build a better future. In the past, both countries allowed their industries to pollute the environment. In the 1980s, they began working together to clean up the air and water and to protect wildlife areas.

The United States and Canada are each the other's top trading partner. This has been the case since major shipping began on the Great Lakes in the 1800s. Each year, more than $40 billion in goods make their way across the border. That makes these two countries the top trading partners in the world. Among the products they exchange are oil, wheat, lumber, and beef.

In 1959, the countries cooperated to build the St. Lawrence Seaway, making it easier for them to trade with each other and also with Europe. The U.S. and Canada agreed to eliminate expensive tariffs on each other's products with the Free Trade Agreement (FTA), which went into effect in 1989. Five years later, the North American Free Trade Agreement (NAFTA) expanded the free trade area to include the U.S.'s neighbor to the south, Mexico.

When two nations have as close a relationship as the U.S. and Canada do, they will always have some disputes. Over the years, the countries have seen eye to eye on most issues, but there have been some notable

The ways in which the U.S. and Canada deal with environmental issues will be an important part of their future. Here, a solar-powered car is being recharged. Solar power is just one possible solution to energy-related problems.

exceptions. For example, although Canada sent troops to aid the peacekeeping efforts of the U.S. in Afghanistan in 2001, its government did not support the U.S. invasion of Iraq in 2003.

What might the future bring? The changing world demands even more cooperation between the two countries. Each will have to make smart decisions in the face of great challenges, including immigration, health care, and the threat of terrorism. After all, when you share a continent and thousands of miles of border, your neighbor's problems can quickly become your own.

Fact File

States of the United States

State	Capital	Population	Area in square miles (sq km)
Alabama	Montgomery	4,599,030	51,718 (133,950)
Alaska	Juneau	670,053	587,878 (1,522,596)
Arizona	Phoenix	6,166,318	114,007 (295,276)
Arkansas	Little Rock	2,810,872	53,183 (137,742)
California	Sacramento	36,457,549	158,648 (410,896)
Colorado	Denver	4,753,377	104,100 (269,618)
Connecticut	Hartford	3,504,809	5,006 (12,966)
Delaware	Dover	853,476	2,026 (5,246)
Florida	Tallahassee	18,089,888	58,681 (151,982)
Georgia	Atlanta	9,363,941	58,930 (152,627)
Hawaii	Honolulu	1,285,498	6,459 (16,729)
Idaho	Boise	1,466,465	83,574 (216,456)
Illinois	Springfield	12,831,970	56,343 (145,928)
Indiana	Indianapolis	6,313,520	36,185 (93,720)
Iowa	Des Moines	2,982,085	56,276 (145,754)
Kansas	Topeka	2,764,075	82,282 (213,110)
Kentucky	Frankfort	4,206,074	40,411 (104,665)
Louisiana	Baton Rouge	4,287,768	47,717 (123,586)
Maine	Augusta	1,321,574	33,128 (85,801)
Maryland	Annapolis	5,615,727	10,455 (27,077)
Massachusetts	Boston	6,437,193	8,262 (21,398)
Michigan	Lansing	10,095,643	58,513 (151,548)
Minnesota	St. Paul	5,167,101	84,397 (218,587)
Mississippi	Jackson	2,910,540	47,695 (123,530)
Missouri	Jefferson City	5,842,713	69,709 (180,546)
Montana	Helena	944,632	147,047 (380,849)
Nebraska	Lincoln	1,768,331	77,359 (200,358)
Nevada	Carson City	2,495,529	110,567 (286,367)
New Hampshire	Concord	1,314,895	9,283 (24,044)
New Jersey	Trenton	8,724,560	7,790 (20,175)

State	Capital	Population	Area in square miles (sq km)
New Mexico	Santa Fe	1,954,599	121,599 (314,939)
New York	Albany	19,306,183	49,112 (127,200)
North Carolina	Raleigh	8,856,505	52,672 (136,421)
North Dakota	Bismarck	635,867	70,704 (183,123)
Ohio	Columbus	11,478,006	41,328 (107,040)
Oklahoma	Oklahoma City	3,579,212	69,903 (181,048
Oregon	Salem	3,700,758	97,052 (251,365)
Pennsylvania	Harrisburg	12,440,621	45,310 (117,351)
Rhode Island	Providence	1,067,610	1,213 (3,142)
South Carolina	Columbia	4,321,249	31,117 (80,593)
South Dakota	Pierre	781,919	77,122 (199,744)
Tennessee	Nashville	6,038,803	42,146 (109,158)
Texas	Austin	23,507,783	266,874 (691,201)
Utah	Salt Lake City	2,550,063	84,905 (219,902)
Vermont	Montpelier	623,908	9,615 (24,903)
Virginia	Richmond	7,642,884	40,598 (105,149)
Washington	Olympia	6,395,798	68,126 (176,446)
West Virginia	Charleston	1,818,470	24,231 (62,759)
Wisconsin	Madison	5,556,506	56,145 (145,414)
Wyoming	Cheyenne	515,004	97,818 (253,349)

Provinces and Territories of Canada

Province/Territory	Capital	Population	Area in square miles (sq km)
Alberta	Edmonton	3,256,800	255,287 (661,190)
British Columbia	Victoria	4,254,500	365,900 (947,800)
Manitoba	Winnipeg	1,177,600	250,947 (649,950)
New Brunswick	Fredericton	752,000	28,355 (73,440)
Newfoundland and Labrador	St. John's	516,000	156,649 (405,720)
Nova Scotia	Halifax	937,900	21,423 (55,490)
Ontario	Toronto	12,541,400	412,581 (1,068,580)
Prince Edward Island	Charlottetown	138,100	2,185 (5,660)
Quebec	Quebec City	7,598,100	594,860 (1,540,680)
Saskatchewan	Regina	994,100	251,866 (652,330)
Northwest Territories	Yellowknife	42,800	501,570 (1,299,070)
Nunavut Territory	Iqaluit	28,300	805,185 (2,093,190)
Yukon Territory	Whitehorse	31,200	186,661 (483,450)

Population figures are for 2006, source the U.S. Census Bureau.

Timeline

c.985	Norse explorer Bjarni Herjolfson records sighting of the North American coastline.
1000	Leif Eriksson lands in Vinland (present-day Labrador or Newfoundland).
1492	Christopher Columbus discovers the Americas.
1497	Explorer John Cabot claims the coast of North America for Great Britain.
1513	Spanish explorer Juan Ponce de León lands in Florida.
1524	Italian explorer Giovanni da Verrazano sails up the east coast of the U.S. and into New York Harbor.
1534	Explorer Jacques Cartier sails into the Gulf of St. Lawrence and claims land for France.
1540	Spanish explorer Francisco de Coronado explores the American Southwest.
1565	Spain establishes the first permanent European settlement in North America in St. Augustine, Florida.
c.1570	The Iroquois Confederacy is formed.
1579	English explorer Francis Drake sails up North America's west coast.
1604	The first permanent European settlement is started in Nova Scotia.
1608	Quebec is founded.
1620	The *Mayflower* lands at Plymouth Rock in present-day Massachusetts.
1626	The Dutch colony of New Amsterdam (present-day New York) is established.
1642	Montreal is founded.
1679	The first European ships sail on the Great Lakes.
1682	LaSalle explores the Mississippi River and claims the territory of Louisiana for France.
1759	Britain takes control of Canada after defeating French forces near Quebec.
1776	The thirteen American colonies declare their independence from Britain.
1791	The U.S. Bill of Rights is ratified.

1803	The U.S. doubles its size with the Louisiana Purchase from France.
1825	The Erie Canal is completed.
1848	Gold is discovered in California.
1857	Queen Victoria chooses Ottawa as Canada's capital.
1861–1865	The Union (northern) and Confederate (southern) states fight the U.S. Civil War.
1863	President Abraham Lincoln issues the Emancipation Proclamation.
1867	Canada becomes a sovereign nation.
1869	The first U.S. transcontinental railroad is completed.
1885	The Canadian Pacific Railway is completed.
1896	The Klondike Gold Rush in the Yukon Territory begins.
1903	The Wright brothers achieve powered flight in Kitty Hawk, North Carolina.
1908	Henry Ford introduces the Model T automobile.
1917	The U.S. and Canada become military allies when the U.S. enters World War I.
1923	Canadian scientists win the Nobel Prize for their discovery of insulin.
1929	The U.S. stock market crashes and the Great Depression begins.
1945	The United Nations is formed in New York City.
1959	Alaska and Hawaii are admitted as the U.S.'s 49th and 50th states.
1964	U.S. Congress passes the Civil Rights Act.
1965	Canada unveils its current Maple Leaf flag.
1967	Thurgood Marshall becomes first African-American U.S. Supreme Court justice.
1969	U.S. astronauts walk on the Moon.
1975	Toronto's CN Tower, the largest freestanding structure in the world, is completed.
1981	Sandra Day O'Connor becomes the first female U.S. Supreme Court justice.
1989	The Free Trade Agreement (FTA) between the U.S. and Canada goes into effect.
1993	Kim Campbell becomes Canada's first female prime minister.
2001	Hijacked airplanes crash into the Pentagon in Washington, D.C., and the World Trade Center in New York City.
2003	U.S.-led forces invade Iraq.
2006	The U.S. Census Bureau estimates that the U.S. population has reached 300 million.

Glossary

arid extremely dry

attorney general chief law officer of a nation

Buddhism religion of Buddhists, based on the teachings of Buddha

colony settlement in a new territory that remains subject to a parent nation

deciduous forest forest in which trees lose their leaves each year

democracy system of government in which citizens select their leaders

desert very dry region with less than 1 inch (25 millimeters) of rainfall per year

domestic having to do with matters within a home country

dominion self-governing territory

ethnic group group defined by characteristics such as race, religious beliefs, or country of origin

exploit to make use of

greenhouse gas gas, such as carbon dioxide, methane, and ozone, that traps the heat of the Sun in Earth's atmosphere

Hinduism religion of Hindus. Hinduism involves a social system and the belief in a divine intelligence called Brahman.

immigration act of entering and settling in a foreign country

indigenous native; having always been in a place

Iroquois confederation of North American Indian tribes, including the Mohawks, Oneidas, Onondagas, Cayugas, Senecas, and Tuscaroras

irrigation supplying water to dry land for agricultural purposes

Islamic related to Islam, the religion of Muslims. Islam is based on the teachings of Muhammad and the Muslim holy book, the Koran.

Judaism religion of Jews, based on the Torah and a belief in one God

megalopolis	very populated area around a city or several cities together
migrated	moved as a group from one area to another
outsourcing	paying outside firms or workers, often in a different country, to perform certain business functions
Pacific Rim	countries around the edge of the Pacific Ocean
persecution	act of unfairly punishing or harrassing a person or group, especially because of race, religion, or gender
province	a territory governed as a political unit within a country. Canada has ten provinces.
service industry	any type of business that provides a service as opposed to goods
subarctic	northern climate with long, bitterly cold winters and short, mild summers
suburb	area near a city where people who work in the city often live
sustainability	ability to meet the needs of a population without overusing resources
tectonic plates	huge sections of rock that form an outer shell around Earth. The plates move slowly and, as they collide, cause earthquakes, volcanoes and the building of mountains.
treaty	agreement between two powers to end a conflict
Tropic of Cancer	imaginary line that marks the northern edge of the tropics
tundra	flat, cold, treeless plain

Find Out More

Further Reading

Bockenhauer, Mark. *National Geographic: Our Fifty States.* Santa Barbara, Calif.: National Geographic Children's Books, 2004.

Braun, Eric. *Canada in Pictures.* Minneapolis: Lerner, 2003.

Little, Catherine, and D'Arcy Little. *The Changing Face of Canada.* Chicago: Raintree, 2003.

Sayre, April Pulley. *Welcome to North America.* Minneapolis: Millbrook, 2003.

State-by-State Atlas. New York: Dorling Kindersley, 2003.

Book Series

State Studies. Chicago: Heinemann Library.
A series of more than 50 books covering each of the United States. Some states have multiple volumes.

Organizations and Websites

www.indians.org
The American Indian Heritage Foundation provides services to Native Americans and builds relationships between native and non-native communities.

www.canada.gc.ca/
The official website of the Canadian government includes just about everything you would want to know about America's northern neighbor.

www.nps.gov
The National Park Service website offers information about all of the U.S. national parks and historic sites.

www.parkscanada.ca
The Parks Canada website shares information about Canada's historic sites and natural wonders.

www.whitehouse.gov
This informative site provides a history of the White House, the presidency, and the U.S. government.

Activities

Here are some topics to research if you want to find out more about the United States and Canada:

Health care
The U.S. and Canada have very different health care systems. What are the strengths and weaknesses of each system?

Immigration
Immigration is a controversial topic in the U.S. today. Research some of the different opinions on immigration.

Climate change
How should the U.S. and Canada begin to address the problem of global climate change? Is this a problem that should be addressed by individuals or by the government?

Index

aerospace industry **48**
African Americans **24, 39**
agriculture **11, 46–47**
Alaska **8, 20, 45, 46, 56**
Alaska Highway **8, 9**
Alberta **45, 47, 57**
Aleutian Islands **20**
Appalachian Mountains **11, 16, 46**
Arctic Ocean **5, 12**
art and entertainment **38–39**
Asian trading links **54**
Atlantic Ocean **12**

baseball **43**
basketball **43**
British Columbia **54, 57**
Buddhism **26, 27**
Bush, George W. **28**

California **6, 24, 56**
Campbell, Kim **30**
Canadian provinces and territories **57**
Canadian Shield **11, 20, 45**
Catholicism **26, 27**
Christian Scientists **26**
Christianity **26, 27**
cities **6, 19, 31, 54**
citizenship **36, 51**
climate **20–21**
climate change **20**
coal **12, 45, 46**
colonialism **8, 26, 28**
Colorado **23, 24, 56**
Commonwealth **29**
culture **24, 34–43**

Death Valley **20**
democracy **28**
deserts **20**
dominion status **29**

earthquakes **12, 17**
education **42, 50**
electoral systems
  Canada **29, 30**
  U.S. **28**
Ellis Island **6**
employment **41, 48, 49, 50–51, 53**
energy requirements **46, 55**
environmental degradation **45, 46, 49, 54**
Erie Canal **15**

fall colors **21**
ferry services **19**
festivals 38, **40**
film industry **39**
First Nations **25**
fishing **13, 19**
Florida **20, 24, 56**
food **40–41, 46**
football **43**

genetically modified foods **46**
grain exports **47**
Great Basin Desert **20**
Great Lakes **12, 46, 54**
Great Migration **24**
Great Plains **11**
Gulf of Mexico **5, 12, 20, 45**

Harlem Renaissance **24**
Harper, Stephen **29**
Hawaiian Islands **5, 18, 20, 56**
health care **26, 41, 50**
  Canada **31**
  U.S. **31**
Hinduism **26, 27**
history of the U.S. and Canada **8–9**
hurricanes **20**

ice hockey **43**
immigration **6, 15, 23, 24, 32–33, 35, 36–37, 50, 54**
illegal **36–37, 51**
indigenous peoples **8, 23, 24–25, 36**
industries **12, 13, 45, 46–49, 50**
Internet **53**
Inuit **36**
iron and steel **12, 45, 46, 48**
Islam **26, 27**
islands **18–19**

Judaism **26, 27**

languages **36**
lumber industry **16, 46, 48**

Mackenzie River **15**
Manhattan Island **18**
minerals **8, 16, 17, 31, 45**
mining industry **45, 46, 48**
Mississippi River **14, 15, 46**
Montreal **6, 25, 38**
Mount St. Helens **17**
mountains **11, 16–17, 18, 20**
music **38–39**

Native Americans **8, 24, 25**
natural gas **45, 46**
natural resources and economy **8, 16, 44–55**
New Orleans **20**
New York City **6, 18, 19, 31, 33, 35**
North American Free Trade Agreement (NAFTA) **54**
Northwest Territory **6, 57**
Nunavut **6, 36, 57**

obesity problem **41**
oil **8, 45, 46**
Olympic Games **42**

Pacific Ocean **12**
physical geography **5, 10–21**
Pier 21, Halifax **6**
political systems
  Canada **29–30**
  U.S. **28–29**
pollution **12, 45, 49, 54**
populations **22–33**
  Canada **5, 6–7, 57**
  mobility **50**
  urban **32–33**
  U.S. **5, 6–7, 56–57**
poutine **40**
poverty **33**
prairie land **11**
Prince Edward Island **18, 57**

Quebec **6, 36, 57**

race and racism **24, 50**
railroads **31, 37, 52**
religions **26–27, 37**
reservations **25**
Revolutionary War **8, 28**
Rice, Condoleezza **30**
Rio Grande **14, 15**
rivers **14–15**
road networks **8, 9, 52, 53**
Rocky Mountains **11, 17**

St. Lawrence Lowlands **11**
St. Lawrence River **12, 15**
St. Lawrence Seaway **15, 54**
San Andreas Fault **12**
science and technology **48–49, 50**
service sector jobs **49, 50**
shipping **12, 15, 31, 54**
slavery **24**
soccer **43**
solar power **55**
sports **42–43**
Statue of Liberty **35**
subarctic region **20**
suburbs and ex-urbs **6, 23, 32, 33**

telecommuting **53**
trade **31, 54**
transportation **12, 15, 19, 37, 52–53**
tropics **20**
tundra **20**

undocumented workers **51**
urban sprawl **6, 53**
U.S. states **56–57**

Vancouver **6, 54**
Vancouver Island **19**
Vermont **21, 57**
volcanoes **17, 18**

War of 1812 **5**
women in government **30**
working life **50**

Yukon **6, 57**